JUL   2012

A GRAPHIC HISTORY OF THE AMERICAN WEST

THE PONY EXPRESS

BY GARY JEFFREY
ILLUSTRATED BY TERRY RILEY

Gareth Stevens
Publishing

Please visit our website, www.garethstevens.com.
For a free color catalog of all our high-quality books,
call toll free 1-800-542-2595 or fax 1-877-542-2596.

Library of Congress Cataloging-in-Publication Data

Jeffrey, Gary.
The Pony Express / Gary Jeffrey.
p. cm. — (A graphic history of the American West)
Includes index.
ISBN 978-1-4339-6749-8 (pbk.)
ISBN 978-1-4339-6750-4 (6-pack)
ISBN 978-1-4339-6747-4 (library binding)
1. Pony express—History—Comic books, strips, etc.—Juvenile literature.
2. Postal service—West (U.S.)—History—19th century—Comic books,
strips, etc.—Juvenile literature. 3. West (U.S.)—History—19th century—
Comic books, strips, etc.—Juvenile literature. I. Title.
HE6375.P65J44 2012
383'.1430978—dc23
2011022833

First Edition

Published in 2012 by
Gareth Stevens Publishing
111 East 14th Street, Suite 349
New York, NY 10003

Designed by David West Books

Photo credits:
p22b, Tom Arthur

Printed in China

CPSIA compliance information: Batch #DW12GS: For further information contact Gareth Stevens, New York, New York at 1-800-542-2595.

CONTENTS

COAST TO COAST

During the gold rush of 1849, hundreds of thousands flocked to California to seek their fortune. The gold rush lasted five short years but helped set up bustling cities and towns that needed to keep in touch with what was happening back East.

California cities like Sacramento carried on growing after the gold rush as people stayed on and set up businesses.

The S.S. California carried mail between the East and West Coasts.

LONG HAUL

Coming by sea, the mail had to travel some thousands of miles up and down Pacific or Atlantic coasts and across land in Panama. The journey could take up to six weeks or longer. Stage companies working overland trails offered to carry passengers and mail between Missouri and California, but their services were neither quick nor reliable.

Mail traveling via stagecoach took more than three weeks at best.

POST TO POST

It was California senator William Gwin who first suggested carrying the post using horseback riders in relays. He suggested to William Russell and his partners of the Central Overland California and Pikes Peak Express Company that if they set up a "Pony Express," they would gain the valuable government mail contract for the West.

The Pony Express guaranteed to deliver the mail in ten days, all year round.

Already in debt, William H. Russell, Alexander Majors, and William B. Wadell gambled that the Pony Express would save their ailing stagecoach business.

Pony Express riders needed to be as light and fearless as jockeys.

Letters cost $5 each to send—very expensive in 1860.

PREMIER SERVICE

A fortune was spent buying the best horses and hiring station tenders and riders. Stations were built from St. Joseph, Missouri, to Sacramento, California. Riders would relay the mail to each other between home stations, using swing stations in between to mount fresh horses. The service began well on April 9, 1860. The mails were delivered on time for four weeks in a row, but then …

THE LONGEST RIDE

UTAH TERRITORY, MAY 6, 1860.

PAIUTE NATIVE AMERICANS HAVE GONE ON THE **WARPATH**. THREE EMPLOYEES OF THE WILLIAMS STAGECOACH STATION ON CARSON RIVER HAVE BEEN **KILLED** AND ITS BUILDINGS PUT TO THE **TORCH**.

THE PYRAMID LAKE WAR HAS **BEGUN**.

MAY 9. AT FRIDAY'S PONY EXPRESS STATION, LAKE TAHOE, BOB HASLAM IS CARRYING THE **EASTBOUND** MAIL 75 MILES (121 KILOMETERS) TO BUCKLANDS STATION...

HA!

...DEEP IN *PAIUTE* TERRITORY.

WHEN HE PULLS INTO *CARSON CITY*...

WHERE IS EVERYONE?

9

EIGHT HOURS LATER...

YAWN – ARE THE MAILS HERE YET?

NOT YET. BUT I GOT SOME CHOW IN THE COOKPOT FOR YOU.

WHEN THE MAIL ARRIVES, HASLAM CARRIES IT WESTBOUND. AS HE APPROACHES COLD SPRINGS, HE GETS THE FEELING...

...SOMETHING'S WRONG HERE.

THEY REACH CARSON SINK TO FIND MEN BARRICADED IN THE BUILDING...

YOU WERE RIGHT TO LEAVE. A WAR PARTY AMBUSHED THE POSSE AND WIPED MOST OF THEM OUT.

HE FINALLY MAKES IT TO BUCKLANDS STATION IN THE DEAD OF NIGHT.

BOY, AM I EVER GLAD TO SEE YOU AGAIN!

WHEW, I'M BEAT!

ONE AND A HALF HOURS LATER, HASLAM SET OUT ON A FRESH HORSE AND REACHED HIS HOME STATION TO HAND THE MOCHILA ON TO THE NEXT RIDER – **THE MAIL HAD GOTTEN THROUGH.**

HE HAD BEEN IN THE SADDLE ON AND OFF FOR NEARLY 30 HOURS, FOR A ROUND TRIP OF 380 MILES (611 KILOMETERS) – THE LONGEST-EVER SINGLE RIDE OF THE PONY EXPRESS.

THE END

STRANGLED BY WIRES

The Paiute war interrupted the service for a month, costing $75,000 in losses. Then Congress agreed to build a new telegraph line between Missouri and California. Only the looming Civil War saved the Pony Express, as the government agreed to keep it going until the telegraph was completed. The promised mail contract never came.

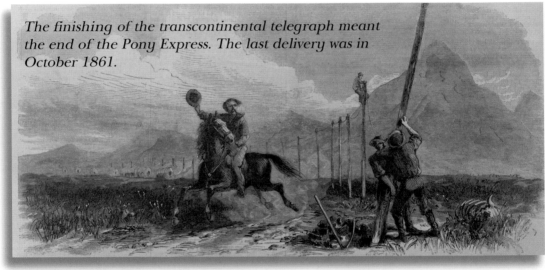

The finishing of the transcontinental telegraph meant the end of the Pony Express. The last delivery was in October 1861.

LEGEND OF THE PONY EXPRESS

One young rider, 14-year-old Will Cody, would go on to form Buffalo Bill's Wild West show. Starting in 1883, the show featured a thrilling reenactment of a Pony Express ride, Native American pursuers and all. This helped the plucky but short-lived venture become one of the most romantic legends of the Old West.

This monument to the Pony Express shows the 1,840-mile (2,961 kilometer) route on its base.

GLOSSARY

ambush To attack suddenly from a hidden place.

barricaded Blocked off for protection or safety from attack.

bustling Full of activity or energy, busy.

deserted Abandoned, without people.

hostiles Enemies or unfriendly people.

lurk Move around secretly, remain in a place sneakily.

mochila A leather pocket attached to the seat of a horse's saddle.

posse A group that assists a sheriff in maintaining order.

pursuer A person who chases or follows after another.

reenactment Acting out an event or situation that happened in the past.

senator A member of the United States Senate who helps make laws.

stagecoach A large horse-drawn carriage used to carry mail or passengers.

suicide ride A trip that will almost definitely lead to harm or even death.

INDEX

A
ambush, 19
Atlantic, 4

B
barricaded, 19
Bucklands Station,
    7, 9, 18–19
Buffalo Bill, 22
bustling, 4

C
California, 4–5, 22
Carson City, 7
Carson River, 6
Carson Sink
    Station, 12, 19
Central Overland
    California and
    Pikes Peak
    Express
    Company, 5
Civil War, 22
Cody, Will, 22
Cold Springs
    Station, 12–13,
    18
Congress, 22

D
deserted, 8

F
Friday's Pony
    Express Station,
    7, 20

G
gold rush, 4
Gwin, William, 5

H
Haslam, Bob, 7–9,
    12–13, 16, 21
hostile, 15, 17

L
Lake Tahoe, 7
looming, 22
lurk, 16

M
Majors, Alexander,
    5
Missouri, 4–5, 22
mochila, 21

N
Native American, 6,
    22

O
Old West, 22

P
Pacific, 4
Paiute, 6–7, 22
Panama, 4
Pony Express, 5,
    21–22
posse, 8, 19
pursuers, 22
Pyramid Lake War,
    6

R
Reeds Station, 8
reenactment, 22
Russell, William, 5

S
Sacramento, 4–5
Sand Springs
    Station, 12, 17
senator, 5
Smith's Creek, 10,
    12
S.S. *California*, 4
stagecoach, 4–5
suicide ride, 10

W
Wadell, William, 5
Williams Stagecoach
    Station, 6